THE QUANTUM NOW

Align Your Energy with Your Purpose
And Live the Life You Dare to Desire

Connie Kean

Title: The Quantum Now: Align Your Energy with Your Purpose And Live the Life You Dare to Desire

By: Connie Kean

ISBN for Print: 979-8-9895409-9-0

Copyright © 2023, Connie Kean

For permissions, contact the author at www.QuantumConnie.com

Cover design: Rhianon Paige

Editing: Dustin Dixon

Published by: AFGO Press

Printed in the United States

First Edition 2023

NOTICE: The information provided in this book is not to be construed as a substitute for medical advice or professional services of any kind. It is for educational purposes only. Neither the author nor the publisher make any representations or warranties, express or implied, about the accuracy, completeness, reliability, suitability, or availability with respect to the information, products, services, or related materials contained in this book for any purpose. The advice and strategies contained herein may not be suitable for your particular situation. Any use of this information is at your own risk.

*This work is dedicated to you, dear Reader,
that you may have the desire to raise your
consciousness, the courage to bring your light
to the world, and the commitment to finding
your way back to the Quantum Now —
because that is all you ever have.*

A NOTE TO THE READER

Dear Reader,

Welcome to the Quantum Now!

Right here, right now. This is where you are. I invite you to remain fully focused in this present moment, on this page, with the sole intention of reading these words.

Take in a slow, deep breath. Now your body is engaged, oxygenated, alert to you, holding you as you are absorbed in the message of this text.

As you breathe in again, imagine one thing you are grateful for. As you hold the image and give thanks, feel the energy of gratitude flood your being.

You are now fully present in this moment with your mental, physical, and emotional energies activated and aligned.

What makes the Quantum Now different from what we tend to think of as the here and now?

It's your focused energy on the smallest measurement of what we call "now" – only 2.5 seconds, according to scientists.

Now is all you have. Everything in this Quantum Now is energy… and so are you.

Yes, you are part of the unified energetic field that is the very fabric of the universe. This Quantum Field of which you are a part is the Source Energy of creation and expansion that is Intelligent and Eternal.

When you understand that everything is energy, including you, the Quantum Now grants you access to the infinite energy of the Quantum Field. When you engage with the Quantum Field, you infuse your life with its Intelligence, Vitality, and Power.

Before we get started, consider taking my **Quantum Now Quiz** to determine where you are energetically at this moment in time so you can then decide how you want to be, energetically speaking, in your life. You'll find the quiz at www.QuantumNowBook.com.

This is the path to both the peace and the joy you seek.

Let's get started.

Connie Kean (a.k.a. Quantum Connie)
November, 2023

TABLE OF CONTENTS

GLOSSARY
OF TERMS

Quantum NOW™ The present moment that cannot be measured by "clock time." It is as short or as long as you are able to be in the energy of the present moment. In the Quantum Now, the human constructs of time and space fall away, giving you access to all time, all space, and all of the possibilities in the Quantum Field.

Quantum Field The unified energetic field that is the very fabric of the Universe. It is the energy of creation and expansion that is intelligent and eternal.

Quantum Eternal Self™ The energetic "forever" part of you that is, always has been, and always will be. It is the quantum aspect of you that transcends time and space. It is the multi-dimensional facet of you that keeps showing up in earthly incarnations (human and otherwise) and can still move between galaxies and dimensions. Some call it their Higher Self, their soul, their spirit, their personal expression of the LifeForce, a spark of God, or the ray of light from Source.

Energetic State The manner or condition of the energy you are expressing (consciously or not) in the Quantum Now.

LifeForce Energy The pure energy of creation that emanates from Source. It is intelligent, ever-expanding, eternal, and infinite. Synonymous with Source Energy.

Source defies definition by our human faculties. Here are some synonyms for Source: The Tao. God. Mother. Father. God. Goddess. The Universe. All That Is. The Intelligent Ever-Emerging Energy of Creation. Universal Intelligence. Cosmic Mind. Light. One Consciousness.

Source Energy The intelligent, creative, expanding, ever-present, pure energy of Source.

Intelligence of the Energy This refers to the omniscience and omnipresence of Source Energy that is available to all of us.

Kinesthetic Intelligence The innate wisdom of your body's energetic systems. It is the intelligence that communicates with your Quantum Eternal Self. It is able to communicate with Mother Earth because it "speaks" the same language. Our life experiences are stored energetically in the body. A Quantum Now Practice teaches you how to communicate with this kinesthetic energy and access its innate intelligence.

Quantum Quickie™ Brief energy exercises that will shift your energetic state in a minute or less.

Auric Field An energy field that exudes out from and surrounds the body. It is called a biofield in the medical model.

The Chakra System A series of 7 large energy centers or Chakras that are connected by a flow of energy that runs through the full length of the body. This flow is called the Pranic Channel in Yogic traditions. We call it the LifeForce Highway as that depicts the many ways the energy can flow up, down, up and down or "North and South" as on a road. The spinning energy centers function like interchanges on a major highway where the LifeForce Energy flows in, out, in and out or "East and West," and all around.

INTRODUCTION

Drowning at 30,000 feet

We're 30,000 feet in the air, and somehow, I'm *drowning*.

It's hours before we land in Singapore. I can't stop coughing, and my lungs are filling up with fluid.

What I thought was bronchitis had turned into pneumonia.

There's a reason my mother pleaded with me not to get on that plane. She knew things could get ugly fast.

And they did.

Had it not been for the angel that was floating on the left side of my head, soothing me and reminding me to take "sips of air," I doubt I would have made it.

Jim and the kids took me directly to the ER when we landed. I was diagnosed with pneumonia, admitted for a week, and given massive doses of antibiotics. After a week of bed rest and medical treatment, I was released to fly home to Jakarta.

Over the course of the next two months, I was prescribed five different antibiotics in an attempt to treat and cure the pneumonia.

I am so grateful to the medical model for saving my life.

However… it could not restore my health, vitality, and signature zest for life.

I longed to get back to living. I wanted my energy back. I wanted to have the energy to be a good parent and a supportive spouse and run my piano studio.

I missed having quality time with Jim and our children. Between my work and his travels to Singapore on a weekly basis, it felt like I had nothing left for the kids except to take care of their most basic needs. There was no ease or fun in my life.

I missed my old, energetic self.

I missed my sharp mind and wit; my brain was working very slowly, and my memory was spotty.

I missed my sense of humor. When that was gone, I knew I was in trouble.

I simply wasn't fun or funny anymore.

My physical health was at an all-time low; it felt like I'd run out of gas. I was too sick to exercise, and my body was losing tone and muscle rapidly. Emotionally, it was a real struggle with wanting to show up for our children (ages four and six at the time) in addition to supporting Jim with his recovery. (I may have forgotten to mention that Jim had a drinking problem.)

Whoopee!

My friend recommended that I try a Reiki treatment. ("A *what* treatment?" I asked.)

At that point, I was willing to try anything, even though any remaining sense of hope was waning fast.

But the moment the Reiki Master "touched" me, I could feel the old Connie start to come back to life: *My* life.

That got my attention, and I immediately knew I had to learn everything I could about this thing called Reiki.

And so began my journey into becoming a Reiki Master, Energy Practitioner, and Quantum Now Teacher.

The Quantum Now is this present moment, here and now, where you direct your energy, intention, and focus. Quantum Energy engages with you because you are energy, too.

When you are fully present in this "now moment," all time and space collapses into the timeless, boundless Quantum Now, giving you access to all possibilities in the Quantum Field.

This may explain why they call me "Quantum Connie."

ॐ

Everything is energy… and so are you.

There are systems of energy inside your body and others surrounding your body.

Even when you die, your energy lives on.

The question is, what kind of energy do you want to *be?* You have the power to decide this, and you can learn how to embody energetic states.

What I learned since meeting that Reiki Master for the first time (her name was Yvonne; I'll never forget it) was that our energy is always shifting. It goes up, it goes down, it goes sideways. And the best part? We can engage with it and direct it.

I'm sure you've heard something like this before, but I need you to pay real close attention here because *the quality of your life depends on it:*

When we fail to understand our own energy and the power we have to align it with our purpose, we will continue to believe that we cannot have what we dare to desire, especially when life doesn't go "as planned."

And when that happens, we lose hope. We lose faith. We lose ourselves.

When I discovered that "everything is energy," I began healing my body. My life not only became *manageable*, but it also became magical.

The Quantum Now Practice has been decades in the making. Through a lifetime of studying, 40+ years of teaching, dedicated spiritual and energetic practices, and the actual *living* of my life, this practice has taught me how to harness the power of my own mind, regulate my energy, and bring peace and functionality into my daily life, even under the most challenging of circumstances.

The Practice takes us into the Quantum Now, where we find peace and stillness in the chaos of our lives, where we have everything, everywhere, *right now.*

It consists of seven energetic states, culminating in One Consciousness.

Here is a brief overview of the seven states:

Energetic State 1: Centering

Getting centered is ground zero. No matter what is happening around you, it is possible to pull yourself and your attention back to the present moment, here and now, where your body is.

Energetic State 2: Connecting

Once you can center yourself, you can connect with your energy and tap into your innate intelligence. This connection to your kinesthetic energy brings grounding, calm, and the ability to make a decision.

Energetic State 3: Communicating

We communicate with so much more than words. We also communicate intuitively, energetically, and physically. Our Auric Field or Biofield constantly interacts with the world around us, expressing our energy outwards. It also collects energy from your environment, engages with your intuition, and translates your physical sensations into useful information.

Energetic State 4: Clearing

The state of Clearing then allows us to let go of what no longer serves us. We remove energetic blockages, lower-vibrating emotions, and the trapped energy of past traumas stored in our bodies.

Energetic State 5: Charging

Like a battery that needs charging, so do your mind, body, and energy systems. You have constant access to the LifeForce Energy. You can plug into it at any time for an instant stream of pure energy.

Energetic State 6: CoExisting

Completely grounded in your body and fueled by the love and wisdom of your highest self, you are able to exist in a symbiotic state with your Quantum Eternal Self, which is the essence of our incarnation into the human experience. This part of oneself moves on when our work here is done. Some call it their Higher Self, their soul, spirit, personal expression of the LifeForce, a spark of God, or the ray of light from Source.

Energetic State 7: Consciousness

In the state we call "consciousness," we have a complete and *judgment-free* understanding of ourselves and the people, places, and things that make up the world around us because we understand it is all energy. We experience loving detachment, the definition of peace.

These seven states represent an expansion of energetic awareness, and they have the power to transform our lives. It is a path from chaos to calm, contraction to expansion, and struggle to peace.

Each state is a "type" of energy we experience as we expand. This is where your power is, and it is good news for anyone who thinks they are always at the mercy of what's happening around them.

Bottom line: you can become your own "energy shifter."

ॐ

The ultimate goal for someone who is just starting down this road is *peace of mind.* It's the kind of peace of mind that comes from having confidence in one's decisions, surroundings, energy, and purpose. Achieving such a mind state is, I believe, the ultimate goal of any energetic being.

My Quantum Now Practice is based on the fact that everything is energy. Yes, that is a scientific fact. No matter how small a particle of matter may be, it is made up of energy that is always in motion. That means you, like me, like the birds, bees, and trees, are *energy.*

This is good news, in case you were wondering. It means we have the power to change our "frequency." The higher the frequency, the "better" we feel. And when we make a conscious effort to raise our frequency, we influence the energy of everyone around us.

As we move through the seven states in the Quantum Now Practice, we raise our frequency.

It's that simple, though not necessarily easy.

But it gets easier with *practice*.

I've had many opportunities to use my Quantum Now Practice since first experimenting with alternative healing methods back when traditional medicine could not cure my pneumonia. That was thirty years ago. Since then, I have learned – from good teachers and through my own self-discipline and practice – that I can shift my *state* within minutes and go from frustrated to functional, from angry to centered, and from hopeless to hopeful by harnessing my power to tap into the innate intelligence we all have.

I certainly didn't know I had it.

I used to have these "feelings" that I should do something or talk to someone. (Now I call it intuition.) When it was time to take action, I would actually argue with myself about whatever I was feeling because it didn't make any sense to me.

Instead of acknowledging my feelings, I shut them down. Time and time again, I realized that if I had followed my feelings, my day would have gone much smoother, if not completely different and better! It took me years to learn to listen to that innate intelligence.

I would argue that having control over your state and knowing how to shift your energy into a calm, peaceful, or productive state is a powerful skill set – the most powerful a human can hope for.

People who come to work with me often tell me, "I am so frustrated with work and with life. I used to be happy and able to get things done. Now I'm exhausted, tired of the pain in my joints, and missing the vibrant relationship I used to have with my partner."

What happened? They are "out of energy" and don't know how to fix it. I'm not talking about merely being tired because you've had a physically exhausting day; I'm talking about being completely zapped of your "life energy." The tank is *empty*, and this can lead to depression, anxiety, and an unrelenting sense of not belonging.

Understanding that everything is energy brings a new way of seeing life. Experiencing the power of that energy in the Quantum Now brings hope and new possibilities for change and healing.

Michelle's Story

Michelle Carter came into my *Quantum Energy Infusion* program with significant childhood trauma that was holding her back from living her best life.

Michelle had high levels of stress and anxiety that were affecting her mental and physical health. Using the Quantum Now Practice, I taught her to release massive amounts of trauma that had been profoundly and subconsciously affecting her life.

As she processed the trauma, Michelle said: "I was able to create space in my life for love and peace to come in." In fact, within a year, Michelle met the love of her life and married him!

In the coming pages, I'll walk you through each of the seven energetic states so you can experience for yourself the "next level" of your life.

You'll find that I have a different approach to energy and healing. Some might say it's quirky, or maybe more appropriately, *quarky*. Nevertheless, there's a reason they call me Quantum Connie!

Let's begin with (the Quantum) NOW.

THE QUANTUM NOW PRACTICE

I lost three dear family members in a year; the most recent was my mom, but my husband and father both passed away in 2022.

One by one, I put them into hospice - at home - and had the privilege of spending the remainder of their human incarnation with them.

My father was first. I traveled to help my mother make the end-of-life decisions for him. We brought him home for his last weeks of care. It was a precious time with both my Mom and Dad as we experienced the joy of family, the power of love, and the preciousness of life.

Throughout this time, I used the Quantum Now Practice to stay fully focused *in the moment* no matter how much grief I felt, how heartbreaking it was to watch my mother say goodbye to the love of her life of 72 years, and being with my daughter and small grandchildren as they came to see their Papa for the last time.

My husband, Jim, courageously lived for two-and-a-half years with 4th stage prostate cancer. I was his caregiver, beloved wife, and energy provider. We believe that all of the energy work he received allowed him to live much longer than expected with low levels of pain until the very end.

Jim believed me when I told him that everything is energy, and so was he! The doctors were constantly amazed by the good quality of his life, given the amount of cancer that was spreading through his bones and lymph system and the intensity of the chemotherapy he endured.

It was hard. All of it. The caregiving, the loving him while losing him, the pain of watching his body disintegrate from the inside out, the physical exhaustion of being a 24/7 caretaker while still working full time, having to support my mother from afar, and keeping the communication channels open with our two adult children to support them through losing their father.

I could not have done any of it without my Quantum Now Practice. I used it hourly as I took care of Jim, ran my company, and grieved the loss of my father.

Then, when I unexpectedly had to put Mom into hospice, it was suffocating, much in the same way that I felt on that airplane three decades before. Once again, my practice saved me as I navigated the hardest moments of my life.

There is one thing that every person in the world has in common, and it is bound up in the energy that we are made of.

I call it the Quantum Now.

A.k.a., the present moment. Right here. Right *now*.

Neuroscientists calculate "now" to be around 2.5 seconds.

The Quantum Now, however, is not measured by time. It is measured by your ability to be in the present moment, with the energy of your mind and body focused only on what is happening for you *right now*.

How do you imagine your life might be different if you were fully present for every moment? What would happen if you didn't get stuck in the past or worry about the future?

Given that all you really have right now *is* right now, how do you want to *live* it?

What do you want to think about right now?

How do you want to feel right now?

What do you want to do right now?

Do you want to think about how you were distracted, mistreated, or derailed yesterday?

Do you want to feel that same frustration right now because you keep thinking about what happened yesterday? Do you want to stay stuck in that kind of energy?

Do you want to take retaliatory action now because of the way you were treated *yesterday?* Are your thoughts spinning out of control, sending your energy in a downward spiral?

The purpose of the Quantum Now Practice is to help you make conscious decisions about how you *want* to think, how you *want* to feel, and how you want to behave in any given "now" moment, for as many moments as you desire.

Like I keep saying, everything is energy. Your thoughts are active energy. Your emotions are energy in motion. They have a frequency that is measured on a scale from low to high.

Emotions that have a low frequency, such as anger, sadness, and fear, vibrate slower than emotions considered to have a higher frequency, such as peace, love, and joy, which vibrate faster.

Your behavior is a function of your frequency.

The choice is all yours.

The power is all yours.

Nothing can change the truth of that.

In other words, at any given moment, you have three decisions to make:

1. What do you want to *think?*
2. How do you want to *feel?*
3. How do you want to *behave?*

Each of those actions has an associated energy that drives, stimulates, and evolves with the decisions you make.

So, what is Energy?

I promise I do not intend this to be a science class, but allow me to briefly describe what I mean by energy.

Energy is constantly moving and vibrating.

When energy vibrates faster, the frequency is considered higher. When energy vibrates slower, the frequency is considered to be lower.

Think of it like this: when you're feeling "down," your energy levels are slow and low.

When you're feeling "up," your energy levels are faster and higher. Have you ever felt yourself actually shake when you were excited or afraid? That is the energy in your body vibrating in overdrive!

Some emotions, such as shame and guilt, vibrate even slower than anger. We can feel lethargic, even depressed at these levels. The higher frequencies of love and joy can bring feelings of lightness, connection, optimism, serenity, and reverence.

Thoughts have vibrations and are energy-activating as well. Your thoughts create emotions, which are energy-in-motion.

All this is to say that unless we get a handle on our thoughts at any given moment, our emotions and behaviors will appear to be beyond our control.

Nothing could be further from the truth.

⁂

To say that I've recently had to practice my own practice would be an understatement. The very recent death of my mother has taken me deep into the Quantum Now Practice.

Over the years, I have taught my students about the importance of living fully in the present moment. When we first begin to contemplate the present moment, it appears to be everything that we can see, hear, taste, touch, and smell.

But there's more. So much more!

The Quantum Now transcends the constructs of time and space. It's what's happening in the Quantum Field, which includes all time and all space right now in this very moment.

Trust me, I know how hard it can be to get your head around that. The fact that you're reading this book tells me you understand more than you may realize.

I have studied with many energy masters, I have learned how to meditate with teachers from different cultures; I know ways to use pranayama or breathwork from multiple systems, different styles of yoga, ways to manifest, methods to lead, rituals to transform, plus other training from my teaching and musical career of 40 years.

Each of these disciplines is valuable in its own right. However, a dynamic synergy occurs when elements of these are used within one system.

For example, working only with energy can leave out the constantly changing dynamics of life.

Having meditation as the main system is blissful until we come out of our meditative state.

Yoga is a beautiful practice while on the mat; however, it does not always result in the same desired state off the mat.

Breathwork is very useful and is a meaningful part of the QNP; however, it is only one part.

The Quantum Now Practice is the synergistic expression of the countless systems that I have studied over the course of my lifetime. It is a simple framework encompassing seven energetic states with specific tools to help you activate each state.

QNP is a way to access these different states of *being* through intention, focus, energy techniques, and daily practice.

In case you might be thinking this is a bunch of gobbledygook, let me put it to you this way: if you feel powerless to change any aspect of your life – whether it's your marriage, relationships with your parents, friendships, your career, your health, your wealth – keep reading because you're going to find out why that is.

I will also show you that you have the power to influence and change every aspect of your life where you want more of the good stuff.

If you're anything like every other human on this planet, you want to feel healthy and strong;

You want to feel special in your relationships;

You want to establish meaningful connections;

You want to feel empowered in your career of choice; You want to be at the top of your game in your career.

You want to feel like you matter;

You want energy still left for YOU at the end of your day.

Most of all, like all of us, you want to feel worthy of all the love in the world. All of that awaits you in the Quantum Field, where endless possibilities exist.

In simple terms, a quantum is the smallest measurable amount of something. It cannot be broken into something smaller. Quantum, for our purposes here, means all that is, here and *now*, unencumbered by the human constructs of linear time and space.

In this Quantum Now, we have access to all possibilities in the Quantum Field.

The Quantum Field is the very fabric of the universe, which includes the Intelligence of expansion and creation. It is this Intelligence and Consciousness that turns the acorn into an oak tree. It determines whether a fertilized egg will become a fox, a sloth, or a unique human being.

It informs whales how to sing their healing songs throughout our oceans. I think of the oceans as being fields of Consciousness, too.

QNP is an opportunity to become fully and completely present in the moment you are experiencing right now, not last week, not ten minutes from now.

This will allow you to assess any given situation, whether it be joyful or terrifying, get centered in your body, mind, and spirit, enter into a state of calm, gather information, make a decision, and then decide what action to take.

In other words, this is how you become everything you wish you could be.

Just because you can't see your energy doesn't mean it's not there.

Your body is energy. Your thoughts are energy.

Everything is energy. And yes – here it comes again –so are you. It's all science.

While quantum physics is beyond the scope of this book, suffice it to say that atoms rule the world! They are the building blocks of our bodies and everything else in the world around us.

Energy is the essence of all that is. It is the Consciousness, the Intelligence, that flows through all of creation.

The **7 Energetic States** in the Quantum Now Practice are a way for you to recognize where your thoughts are and the state of your mind at any given moment. *See figure below.*

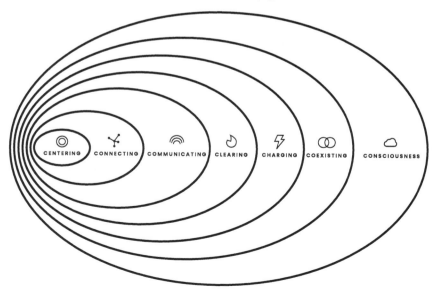

Energetic State 1, where we learn to **CENTER,** is the easiest to learn. We all have an idea of what it means to "regroup" and center ourselves when we get thrown for a loop. In the midst of a scattered, fragmented, emotionally charged, painful, mentally foggy, or fight-or-flight moment, your job is to find your center and stay in the present moment.

Once you can gather yourself, you can **CONNECT** with your energy and tap into your kinesthetic intelligence, which combines your physical energy and the wisdom of your Quantum Eternal Self. It allows you to tap into your decision-making capabilities.

Now you're able to **COMMUNICATE** with the Quantum Field (the energy you cannot see) through your Auric Field. It gathers information from your environment, engages with your intuition, and translates your physical sensations into information.

The energetic state of **CLEARING** allows us to release what no longer serves us. Energy is neither created nor destroyed, so it is important for us to release lower vibrating energies and blockages from our bodies and energy systems.

The energetic state of **CHARGING** is where we bring LifeForce or Source Energy into our body and energy systems.

The energetic state of **COEXISTING** happens when we are fully grounded in our body and simultaneously able to engage with the Intelligence of the Energy through our Quantum Eternal Self. It brings inner harmony, peace, knowingness, and compassion.

And finally, as we reach the seventh energetic state of

CONSCIOUSNESS, we are able to raise our frequency or energetic awareness to a vibrational state of love, joy, peace, gratitude, bliss, oneness, nirvana, and enlightenment.

This process of moving through each of the seven energetic states gives us access to our subconscious, where most of our past traumas, old conditioning, and limiting beliefs reside.

Using the body's innate intelligence, we can bring this information forth to our conscious mind so we can examine it, release it, bless it, or integrate it into our current ways of being. This helps us access our thoughts and emotions so we can make better-informed decisions that affect our behavior and then our outcomes.

It is possible to have a huge shift in your day/life/situation by consciously centering your energy (the first energetic state). I have done many difficult things in my life just by remaining centered.

Each energetic state *expands* into the next.

As you develop your Quantum Now Practice, you will find yourself naturally flowing from one state to the next.

Let me show you what I mean.

ENERGETIC STATE 1:

Centering

My mother died unexpectedly while I was writing this book.

I was blindsided with shock, disbelief, and immeasurable grief.

I want to use my personal experience to show you how one can move through the seven energetic states, no matter how trying or impossible the circumstances may seem, by getting centered, clearing out the bad energy, charging yourself up with the good, and reaching states of equilibrium, acceptance, and divine guidance.

Thank goodness I had this system in place to get me through the whole ordeal – from the initial shocking and soul-crushing sadness, long hours in the hospital, and endless decisions – to the massive amount of work that had to be done to liquidate my mother's estate.

Amidst the chaos that ensued, the only thing I could manage to do in any given moment was to remind myself to "center."

In the beginning, it felt like I was drowning in panic; it reminded me of my experience on that plane thirty years ago. Like back then, I noticed that life didn't stop and wait for me to pull myself together. In fact, it can often feel like we're playing a bad game of whack-a-mole.

But how do we do this? How do we get ourselves back into a state of equilibrium so we can begin to think clearly?

First and foremost, we remind ourselves that we have a toolkit comprising of seven Energetic States.

Energetic State 1 is the hammer in our toolkit because it is the most basic of tools. It brings us back to Center, which is always available to us.

Centering ourselves energetically allows us to be present and grounded in our bodies.

Returning ourselves to Center is how we come into the present moment, again and again, *and again.* That's why we call this a *practice.* It is a seemingly never-ending practice of watching our mind run off and then gently pulling it back to Center.

We have a powerful flow of energy that runs right down the middle of our body. I call it the LifeForce Highway. When we center ourselves, we tap into that massive energy system that gives us a boost and helps ground our energy.

None of the other Energetic States will work if you try to skip this one.

It's like trying to hammer a nail with a screwdriver.

Everything begins with Centering.

❧

It was late in the evening when my phone rang.

Pete, my mom's friend, begged, "Connie, pray for your Mom, and I need you to send her some energy right now."

"What's wrong?"

"Your mom has fallen, and her heart has stopped."

"What happened?"

"We don't know. Dr. Katchem is giving her CPR. We've called 911."

Click.

I stood in my bedroom, in the dark, in a state of shock. I felt like a giant wrecking ball had just knocked all of the wind and the life out of me.

I was numb.

Send your mom some energy...

I had to do something, but I was paralyzed and suffocating.

Get centered. *Take a breath.*

Get centered. *Take another breath.*

Get centered. *Now I'm back in my body.*

I start to send Mom some energy. Because I am centered, I can tap into the powerful LifeForce Highway that runs through my body.

Centering is all I can do in this Quantum Now. It allows me to be a part of my mother's experience 1000 miles away by sending her energy. I am an energy practitioner, and I know there are more states. However, in this moment of shock, despair, and grief, I recognize that I must be able to help myself before I can be in the right energetic state to extend help to my beloved mother in the form of an energy treatment.

Everything is Energy.

I am energy.

Center yourself, Connie.

With this foundation rediscovered and freshly cemented, I would attempt to take the next crucial step in my Quantum Now Practice: Connecting.

ENERGETIC STATE 2:

Connecting

Life's ups and downs can constrict and contract our energy, leaving us feeling stuck, tired, sad, lost, brain-fogged, or depressed. That's why we need to have a system in place so we can shift our energy and actually change our energetic state, which leads to expanded states of being with peace, flow, improved energy, and mental clarity.

I designed my Quantum Now Practice to teach my students how to use their energy to work *with* and *for* them. This skill can improve the quality of your life without having to rely on outside forces to do it for you.

Once we can center ourselves, we are ready for the Energetic State I call **Connecting**. This can only occur if we are able to be present in our bodies by Centering.

The higher the energetic state, the more "effective" we can be in our lives. Our goal is to be able to access the power and wisdom of our kinesthetic intelligence, which has an unlimited amount of energy associated with it.

Achieving Energetic State 2 requires us to access a combination of our physical energy and the wisdom of our Quantum Eternal Self.

After receiving news that my mother was clinging to life, I knew I had to manage my mental and emotional states, or I wouldn't be able to help her, let alone myself. This is much easier to teach than to do when the life of someone you love hangs in the balance, so I really had to work on it.

This meant I had to get to her!

My heart was broken, and my mind was shut down, but I still needed to be with her to help her, comfort her, and let her know how much I loved her. In spite of the shock reverberating through my body and mind, I was still able to get centered and move to be connected so I could make a decision about booking a flight to be by her side in Illinois.

I tapped into the wisdom of my body to tell me what to do.

The message that came through to me: *Book the 5 o'clock flight, Connie.*

I thanked my body's kinesthetic intelligence for saving my seemingly incapacitated brain from having to stress over the travel details.

Have you ever felt so helpless? We all have.

Have you ever felt that the situation you were in was utterly hopeless?

The truth is, we are never helpless, and the situation is never hopeless if we know how to change our energetic state.

But not knowing how to change our state so we can access the Quantum Now means we end up living life being controlled by the thoughts and emotions generated by circumstances and people outside of ourselves.

We cannot see how we are connected until we understand that everything is energy, even you (and me!).

We are unable to see that we are all part of the same web of life. The consequences of this lack of understanding are what create the reality we *don't* want – the life we don't want.

In other words, we end up shirking our responsibility to live a life of "energetic harmony," which sucks our energy away from our goals, dreams, and passions.

A life of low, incoherent energy can result in physical pain, brain fog, and runaway emotions.

This is what happens when we fail to step into the Quantum Now.

So, let's start communicating.

ENERGETIC STATE 3:

Communicating

We've talked a bit about what it means to center ourselves in our body, tapping into the energy highway that runs through us so we can access the LifeForce Energy available to all of us.

It also means connecting to the energy and wisdom of our Quantum Eternal Self and the kinesthetic intelligence of our body to give us the ability to make decisions even when we are in distress.

For example, the doctor woke me up at 5 a.m. the very next morning, asking me what to do about a DNR (Do Not Resuscitate) order. I had to clear my head and make a life-or-death decision regarding my beloved mother.

But I was exhausted. And heart-broken. My mind was clouded. My emotions coursed through me like I was holding an electric fence.

If I was ever going to be able to make a decision affecting my mother's life, I'd better check my energetic state.

Get centered, Connie. (Check.)

Connect with your body's wisdom, Connie. (Check.)

Connecting to my Quantum Eternal Self allowed me to make life-altering decisions for my mother because I could then enter the Energetic State of **Communicating.**

The skill required to master this third state is the ability to use our Auric Field to energetically express ourselves outward, gather the information we need from our environment, engage with our intuition, and finally translate our physical sensations into information we can use in the moment to deal with whatever situation is before us.

My mother was literally unconscious, and I was naturally feeling lost, alone, and overwhelmed. The goal wasn't to *not* feel anything but rather to acknowledge and process my emotions so they didn't unravel me completely.

However, should you ever unravel, remind yourself to start at the beginning by Centering and work your way up the energy ladder.

We all have an Auric Field, which is our energy emanating from that LifeForce Highway inside us. Our Auric Field extends onto the Quantum Field, where we live and move. Our Auric Field and the Quantum Field speak the same energy language.

We can literally communicate with the entire unified field that is the very fabric of the universe! We can think of it as consciousness, too; that the field is conscious, as are we, so we can communicate at that higher level.

The easiest way for me to communicate with my Auric Field is to do the Infinity Weave. It is a simple Quantum Quickie that can clear, strengthen, harmonize, and extend your personal energy field. Energy moves in patterns, and one of Its favorites is the figure 8, also known as the infinity symbol.

Moving your hand in your field in the shape of the infinity sign reinforces the energy already moving in that pattern. It helps strengthen the density of your field. It also enlarges the size of your field. It aids the kinesthetic intelligence of your body in communicating with your biofield because your arms, hands, and fingers can feel the energy of your field as you move through it and vice versa!

The Infinity Weave also encourages your Auric Field to interact with the Quantum Field.

Do you see all of the levels of communication taking place here?!

Now, here's what this all means in simple terms: You don't have to *think* about any of this. Your brain is not engaged when we are in the energetic state of Communicating – your biofield is communicating with the Quantum Field – you're speaking an entirely different energetic "language" of intuition and physical sensations (kinesthetic intelligence.)

I engage with my intuition by moving out of my brain into my heart center or my third eye center. Shutting down my conscious mind allows the rest of my body, energy, and intuition to activate.

If this sounds complicated, don't worry. At this point, all that you need to understand is that a lot of things are energetically happening to us, whether we're aware of it or not.

This book aims to raise your energetic awareness, even if it doesn't all make sense right now. Raising your awareness will help you understand the cause of your suffering.

Without understanding how to access the State of Communication, we end up adding to our suffering, not relieving it.

So much suffering comes from our old thoughts going 'round and 'round in our heads. Being stuck in a loop like this only adds to our anguish and does not allow us to get to a different state where we can see our situation in a new way.

This is why we can feel paralyzed by the intensity of the emotion (grief, anxiety, loneliness, stress, heartbreak, loss, fear, etc).

As I faced the decision presented to me by my mother's doctors, I was able to see clearly what my mother would have wanted (respect the DNR) rather than telling doctors to do whatever it took to keep her alive.

It's not that I didn't feel immense sadness; it's that I didn't allow this emotion to dictate my actions. My intuition guided me.

It's important to develop the skills of listening to your intuition so you can confidently enter into the next Energetic State of Clearing, which is all about releasing the old, stored, resistant, trapped, clingy, blocked, sludgy, sticky energy that no longer serves you.

ENERGETIC STATE 4:

Clearing

Since the human body is made up of atoms (protons, neutrons, and electrons), we are energy *personified*. Understanding this allows us to tap into this higher source of intelligence within each of us.

Remember, *everything* is energy, and everyone is energy.

Being in an energetic state of **Clearing** means you are able to release the energy of emotions that don't allow you to feel at the top of your game. In other words, if you can identify emotions and the energy that drives them, you can change the way you feel.

It's like running your feelings through a washing machine.

You may have heard of various ways you can do this: through meditation, calming music, eating well, sleeping more, etc.

However, a Quantum Now Practice will take you further because it trains you to clear the energy and keep it out effectively. Have you ever experienced a yoga class that left you feeling invigorated and at peace, only to feel the stress of your life come roaring back within hours after leaving the class?

The work we are doing here is designed to bring you sustained peace, calm, and balance even in difficult times. You are acquiring the tools to create "calm on demand" when all else is out of your control.

It allows you to regain some semblance of order over your emotions in spite of the chaos around you.

When you are in an energetic state of Clearing, you will feel lighter and more energized. You may also notice that you are more positive and optimistic. Our goal is to practice extending this energetic state minute by minute, hour by hour, day by day, week by week.

This is an ongoing practice that takes place no matter what is going on in your life.

As things became increasingly dire for my mother, I sensed my mind wanting to go in several directions. By now, I was at the hospital. The trauma doctor showed me a new CT scan that revealed that the small brain bleed from her fall had spread across the entire right hemisphere of her brain. The doctor offered a surgical procedure that would cut out part of my mother's skull to relieve the pressure in her head.

I wanted time to stop. Shock and disbelief enveloped me.

End-of-life decisions had to be made quickly, and I simply did NOT want to have to make them. There were times when it was hard enough to stay *centered*, let alone get myself to an energetic state of Clearing.

How was I supposed to give the doctor a clear-headed, open-hearted answer as my mother's advocate? I asked the doctor for a little time alone with Mom to make this decision. I immediately started to clear out the energy of chaos in my mind and the emotional pain in my heart.

Entering a state of clearing allows us to release what no longer serves us. Energy is neither created nor destroyed, so it is important for us to release or transmute lower vibrating energies and blockages from the body and its energy systems.

I found myself experiencing emotions that covered the full range of frequencies, from high-vibrating unconditional love for Mom to low-vibrating hopelessness and despair.

When I intentionally process painful, traumatic, unbearable emotions as they arise, they do NOT have to get stuck in my energy systems or stored in my body.

This is the point of magic in the work.

This is where we can change the normal human way of repressing emotions, burying trauma, and shoving down our feelings because we honestly do not know how to deal with them. Most of us do not have a system in place to acknowledge, honor, and process the emotions of life as they arise.

I use several techniques to help release energy that would otherwise remain stuck in the body. I invite you to visit my website, where I have a series of videos to share with you. Go to QuantumNowBook.com.

Without the ability to release this energy, we end up a prisoner of our uncontrolled responses to an unimaginable turn of events in our lives. Our hearts are shattered, and we have no mental capacity to reason our way out of it. We are at the mercy of a flood of biochemical reactions cascading through our bodies from the trauma.

We simply cannot get a grip on our bodies, minds, or emotions. However, when we learn to release these emotions, we experience a sense of relief that comes with feeling in control of our actions, even though we have no control over our circumstances.

It gives us strength.

If you've ever felt like you've been traumatized by life's circumstances and couldn't figure out how you were ever going to be okay again, it's because you haven't yet learned how to enter the energetic state of Clearing.

Or maybe you've learned to do this without even realizing it. Have you ever exercised to exhaustion? Have you ever "let it all out" to a therapist? Going on a long run, crying yourself to sleep, or screaming into a pillow will also get us there.

There are many other ways to clear energy: yoga, martial arts, dancing, going to the gym, or having coffee with a trusted friend.

But sometimes those activities aren't available at a moment's notice; The Quantum Now, however, is *always* available to you. You can effectively clear this energy from your system while it's happening, no matter what is happening around you.

Consciously clearing unwanted emotions so they don't remain

trapped in our bodies is the gift of this 4th energetic state.

I've watched my students move massive amounts of traumatic energy in group sessions I teach, but they also learn to do it on their own. In fact, I teach my students to make this part of their daily practice.

The hardest work is done. In the Quantum Now, you are ready for a charge that brings restoration, vitality, and hope.

Having cleared the path for life-giving energy to enter our heart, mind, body, and soul, we are now prepared to enter the Energetic State of Charging.

ENERGETIC STATE 5:

Charging

The consequences of not understanding that *everything is energy* can be dire.

I don't mean to be dramatic, but we see this all the time: people living in constant states of low-vibrating emotions such as shame, humiliation, despair, regret, fear, anxiety, or anger.

When we spend our days living in and sending out these heavy energies, we create our reality at a lower level of possibilities. We attract other low-vibrating people, circumstances, and experiences into our sphere.

This can be felt as dishonesty in business dealings, disrespect in relationships, being ignored in the workplace, gang mentality, fear for safety, being shamed or humiliated, or experiencing injustice of any kind.

The cost of maintaining the status quo is that you will never know the power, peace, and utter *magic* available to you when you understand that *everything* is energy, even *you*.

We all face difficult daily situations that can knock us out of balance and leave us frustrated, angry, or even helpless.

The State of **Charging** brings LifeForce back into your body and its energy systems.

We have access to Source Energy at all times.

Not knowing or understanding this can leave us in a state of physical exhaustion, mental fogginess, emotional distress, unhappiness, fearfulness, desperation, or full of shame. (Have I left anything out?)

This is when we most need a charge.

That's easier said than done, I'll admit. Between the shock, trauma, lack of sleep, and end-of-life decisions I had to make on behalf of my mother, I was exhausted and heartbroken.

It took some effort, but I was able to use the tools in my Quantum Now toolkit to charge up my energy systems to help my bone-tired body, frazzled mind, and broken heart realign themselves with the Earth.

The Earth has a natural frequency of 7.83 Hz. Not coincidentally, so do humans.

We feel centered when aligned with the Earth's electromagnetic field (State 1). One of the benefits of this alignment is stress tolerance, of which I was in desperate need.

It's a frequency that rejuvenates us on every level.

That's why "becoming one with nature" is so powerful... it

naturally recharges us.

Without awareness (or being "centered"), we can walk in the park all day long and never get to any of the energetic states because our mind is cluttered with stressful thoughts that block our body's natural attempts to align itself with the Earth's natural frequency.

I recall playing in a park with my young children in the shade of a large tree. I leaned back to relax against its huge trunk, and I felt a wave of energy run up my back. This was early in my study of Reiki, so I understood energy at a basic level. It surprised me that a tree would energetically reach out to me.

I decided to open up my Reiki energy to the tree. What ensued was a gentle, lovely, mutual exchange of energy that felt like a warm tree hug. The frequency of the earth not only resonates with our bodies, but it is intelligent and speaks the same energetic language.

Everything is Energy, even the trees!

Not until we clear unwanted energy, or what I like to call karmic sludge, are we able to charge our systems with the LifeForce Energy that is required for the next state in the Quantum Now Practice.

The Chakra Charge is an effective way to bring the LifeForce Energy into the body and energy systems. By spreading out the arms and throwing the head back, it expands the chest, which activates the heart chakra. The energy enters into the heart, throat, and 3rd eye chakras as they are opened up by the wide-flung posture of the body.

Having the intention to fill your chakra system with LifeForce Energy alerts the intelligence of the chakras to join in on the exercise. Once the 4th, 5th, and 6th Chakras are engaged, the 7th chakra lights right up!

Ensuring the feet are grounded is important to keep the LifeForce Energy flowing from the heart through the lower chakras to the soles of the feet and right into the earth.

This engagement with the earth helps pull the energy downwards, activating the 3rd, 2nd, and 1st chakras.

This activity also grounds the LifeForce Energy into the earth, which, in turn, feeds and invigorates Mother Earth. *This* is the LifeForce Highway that runs from Source Energy right through you, into the Earth, and all the way back up again!

It is a constant flow of energy.

This Quantum Quickie mobilizes the entire Chakra System, enlivening the body, stimulating the mind, and sparking intuition.

The Chakra Charge benefits everyone, from beginning students to more experienced energy practitioners.

Having the Chakra System mobilized helps set us up for the next Energetic State we call CoExisting.

ENERGETIC STATE 6:

CoExisting

When you are in the state of **CoExisting**, you are fully engaged with your Quantum Eternal Self while fully grounded in your body (your *human* self).

This dance between your soul and your psyche is the most critical aspect of CoExisting.

It's where we learn that it is not only possible to be a soul having a human experience but that it's also possible to live life both fully human and *fully* divine. It is the State of CoExisting that brings this forth in a way in which you can exist in an expanded state and still buy groceries.

It is up to each one of us as embodied humans to make this connection with our Quantum Eternal Self. The hope is then to operate from this expanded version of you with access to Universal Intelligence.

You must have a strong desire for this connection to bring it forth because it is not how we have been programmed to live as human beings. We have been operating from our personality structures (the ego) our whole lives. It requires a seismic shift to move away from old habits and the pull of the human personality to the wisdom of the Quantum Eternal Self.

CoExisting begins with you, inside of you, despite you!

CoExisting between your psyche and your higher self must happen at the individual level first. This coexistence then expands outwards to those close to you. They are your training ground – the relationships that trigger you the most, no matter how much you love them, are where your deepest inner work can happen.

This shift into coexistence requires disciplined dedication to do the deep work, the awareness to see yourself, the courage to change, and the patience and grace to gift yourself as you begin and fail and begin (and fail) yet again.

It requires a whole lot of unconditional love.

Balancing my Chakras has been an effective way for me to move into the State of CoExisting. Of the seven main chakras in the body, the upper three are our spiritual energy centers, with the lower three being our physical energy centers. The heart center in between is where the spiritual and the physical energies meet, mix, coexist, and express outwards as us; that is, the human and the divine intertwined.

Balancing the chakras can put us in a State of CoExistence because we bring a physical and a spiritual chakra into balance or harmony.

The frequency of CoExistence is a high frequency of pure love and light.

It is the state that brings our human self and our higher self into alignment.

It is the state that unites us all.

It is a state of forgiveness and deep healing.

It is the ultimate state of tolerance and acceptance.

When you are in this Energetic State, you are able to CoExist in the same space as others without disrupting their energy fields.

Of course, the best space to be in is one where everyone is in a State of CoExisting, where each person is responsible for their own energetic field.

There is a deep respect for other people's boundaries and their right to be whoever and however they choose to be.

When we are in this energetic state, we create harmony and peace for ourselves and the people we love, even when we disagree with them. We honor our own experience, and we respect the experiences of others, no matter what energetic state they are in.

This is where we strive to *be*.

It is a state of kindness and compassion.

It is a state of allowing and acceptance.

It is a state of gratitude and grace.

It is a state of giving and taking with love.

❧

Back in my early days of self-discovery, I was reeling from the tragic death of my 21-year-old brother Bobby in a car accident. Amid the paralyzing shock and trauma, my parents were unable to attend to the funeral arrangements. At the young age of 22, I was in charge of everything. I was overwhelmed by grief and yet comforted by some other-worldly presence feeding me ideas and giving me the sheer will to keep going, somehow.

I was in a small airplane the first time I "saw" Bobby *after* he had died. It was right after the funeral, and I felt like I had been flown up to the heavens to be near him in that tiny Cessna. I saw him gently playing with a young child on his lap. Children loved Bobby, and that had not changed on the other side. It brought me joy and great peace to feel his presence so clearly and powerfully.

Bobby came to me often in my dreams, and I woke up knowing we had just been together in some other realm. It occurred to me that if I could connect with a soul who was no longer in the physical, I could certainly connect with anyone inhabiting a human body. It helped me understand the coexistence of all souls, no matter our location.

Because of this life experience as a young adult, I became a seeker of answers to deep philosophical questions about life after death, communication with other realms, dimensions, and heaven, and why bad things happen to people. It certainly expanded my worldview, ESP, and intuition.

You have undoubtedly experienced this, too, even though

you may not be aware of it. Have you ever had an experience meeting a person for the first time, yet you feel as though you know them?

Have you ever felt deeply connected to something or someone you just saw on the news?

Have you felt a tremendous amount of compassion for your friend who is experiencing hardship?

Does your heart go out to a victim of injustice?

Have you ever felt so much love that you felt bigger than yourself? Was it on your wedding day? Was it when your child was born?

If so, you now know what it means to CoExist.

❧

I entered the energetic state of CoExisting right before my mother crossed over.

It's as though I moved into this state naturally and willingly, as if another side of me welcomed me with open arms.

Was this my mother's energy coexisting with mine?

I could hear her, as I did on that day when she told me not to get on that airplane.

On this day, the day before she died, she was telling me that it was time for her to go. She really wanted me to know that she was ready to leave. She knew that I was going to be okay and, in fact, thrive with more time for myself.

I could feel her loving me unconditionally, wanting the best for me.

I could also feel the parts of me that did not want to let her go. We had just spent the winter together in Florida. I discovered parts of my mother that I never knew existed!

We loved being together day after day, having morning coffee, sharing meals, and talking when I was done with work. Mom got to see me in action with my company and finally understood what I had created. It was so much fun to share it with her!

Resistance only made the pain of loss worse… I couldn't believe that we were not going to have any more winters together.

I had to let it go.

I had to let her go.

I used all of my QNP energy techniques to process the deep pain I was feeling.

When we enter the Energetic State of CoExisting, we give ourselves the gift of expansion.

Energetically, we are a vast multi-layered version of ourselves plugged into Source Energy through our Quantum Eternal Self and still firmly grounded on earth in our human bodies.

We open ourselves up to new beginnings, new possibilities, and new opportunities for personal and professional growth, deeper relationships, and a joy like we've never known.

And here's the best part: When we are in the energetic state of CoExisting, we don't only affect the present moment; we create a better world for ourselves, our loved ones, and future generations.

We are raising the collective consciousness to a State of Peaceful CoExistence.

ENERGETIC STATE 7:

Consciousness

Nirvana? Enlightenment? Complete and utter bliss?

What is this energetic state we call **Consciousness?**

One thing we know for sure: it is a state that is available to any of us who choose to do the inner work to raise our frequency and energetic awareness to a vibrational state of love, joy, peace, gratitude, oneness, nirvana, enlightenment or *complete and utter bliss.*

Much has been written about what it means to be "conscious," and much remains unknown. Some take the position that it is not simply an energetic state but a more complex phenomenon that we may not be capable of understanding at the human level. In other words, the concept of consciousness is BIG.

But rather than getting ourselves bogged down in science and physics and such, for purposes of our Quantum Now Practice, I define the *Energetic State* of Consciousness as being "One With The Field." This is a human peak state we experience by energetically communing with the One Consciousness, a synonym for Source.

In this Energetic State, I have full awareness that I am energy, that everything is energy, and that I am one with all living beings, one with Earth, one with humanity.

We live in a unified energy field.

I acknowledge that the energy of the field is running through me.

When I experience being One With The Field, it feels like the density of my body dissipates into the Quantum Field. What is left – my consciousness and my energy field – merges with the One Consciousness of the Quantum Field, the very fabric and Intelligence of the Universe.

This is the ultimate state of the Quantum Now Practice!

State 7 is what I desire to reach during my morning ritual of balancing my chakras, breathwork, praying, and meditating. Again, the 7th Energetic State of Consciousness is an elevated, expanded human state that aligns us with the One Consciousness.

It does not happen every day, though. With continued practice, I hope to reach a level of mastery where I can count on it daily. What does happen every minute of every day is the Quantum NOW, the moment when we connect to the energy of everything that has ever been and will be in the smallest possible quantity of time, the present moment.

Practice, practice, practice.

This is a lifelong journey that we must revisit and practice time and again, no matter which energetic state we attain that day.

It's why we call this the Quantum Now Practice.

⁂

During the first days of Mom's hospitalization, I was unable to reach the energetic state of Consciousness.

It was all I could do to get to Centering and Connecting to handle the simplest tasks of getting dressed, praying for Mom, booking a plane ticket, packing a suitcase, and flying to Illinois.

Hour by hour, with each heart-wrenching decision I had to make, I was able to be in the Quantum Now by Centering, Connecting, and eventually, Communicating.

Eventually, I was able to stretch myself to the 4th State of Clearing to release some of the crushing grief from my chest so I could breathe.

Day by day, the State of Charging brought Source Energy to resurrect my depleted body. Decision after decision, I was able to access the power and intelligence of the Quantum Now.

I have to admit, though, it was hard. It was hard to access the Quantum Now because the loss was so fresh. My energies were understandably chaotic at that time. My mind wanted to take me back to the past, where I had my mom, and forward into the future, where she was no longer with me.

I needed to practice.

I eventually found myself in the Quantum Now, fully present. Time and space vanished. It was in the final days, once my mother was in hospice in her home, that I was able to sit and practice long enough to access the state of Consciousness.

When I was sleeping in a "real bed" at Mom's house, I was able to reinstate my morning energy-prayer-meditation-breathwork practice, which, most days, invokes the State of Consciousness for me. I was so grateful for this return because it feeds the deepest *soul* part of me in a way that human life does not.

When we are "unconscious" (not present), we forget the vastness of life. We constrict ourselves into old patterns of trauma. We're stuck in habitual personality traits. We feel fearful, unloveable, not enough, unworthy, and unsafe.

We forget that we don't have to do it all by ourselves.

We forget that love is everywhere and that the frequency of love vibrates throughout the Quantum Field.

When I go unconscious – in other words, I allow my mind to run free – I think too much. My monkey mind takes over the knowingness of my heart and hijacks the intelligence of my intuition. My mind gets louder and louder, distracting me from my vision and the important work at hand. I feel scattered and ineffective.

Merging my consciousness with the One Consciousness disengages my human mind, plugs me into Source Energy, and grants me full access to it. After this, I am able to bring the knowingness of being One With The Field to whatever is in front of me.

When I am in this State, I'm in the flow. It feels like I have access to everything I need, knowing that my life is unfolding in a Quantum Field of Intelligent Creative Energy.

It feels like I am supported and nurtured by the Universe in ways I cannot explain.

It feels magical.

It feels stable.

It feels fluid.

It feels safe.

I remind myself to ride the waves of ever-expanding energy as if I were "hanging 10" on the front wave of human evolution into the New Earth.

NEXT STEPS

I am proud to say I now have decades of study under my belt, but the biggest, most important lesson is this: *I had the power all along but didn't know how to access it.*

I didn't know that everything is energy; that I am energy!

I didn't know that *all I had to do* was ground myself into a centered state, thereby enabling me to access the part of me that knew what to do at any given moment.

The Quantum Now Practice is a way to access different states of being through intention, energy techniques, and daily practice. It gives you a step-by-step process to engage with the Intelligence, vitality, and power of the Quantum Field.

By now, you might be thinking that maybe everything could be energy.

Really, though? I mean, *IF* this is true, why hasn't anyone ever told you this before?

Since you are still reading, some of you must be curious about all these energy ideas. So, the question now becomes: what are you going to do with this curiosity?

Here are the consequences of putting this book down and doing nothing differently in your life:

- You stay in a seemingly constant state of anxiety and stress because you don't know how to dial up or dial down your energetic frequency;
- You ignore the health of your body; you think your body is somehow separate from you and therefore don't take responsibility for taking care of it;
- You spend less time with your friends; you are so busy you can't seem to get a grip on your time to do things for yourself or get to the meetings where your people gather or to the events that feed you;
- You see the environment as separate from you; you don't see how when the environment suffers, you suffer, the people you love suffer;
- You are far more likely to engage in self-destructive behaviors because you fail to see your impact on others and the world at large.
- You are detached from the very people who nurture you because you don't feel like yourself; you don't know what's wrong, and you don't even know who you can discuss it with - it all sounds and feels crazy;
- You will choose to separate yourself from loved ones because of an inability to connect with yourself.

There is a price to pay when we fail to see that we are part of something unfathomably bigger than ourselves.

You might be thinking that this everything is energy thing is just *too far out there.*

Heck, I can't even see energy; how can it be everything?

My friends will think I've lost my mind with all of this energy talk.

My partner won't even want to hear it, let alone have a conversation about it.

Or maybe you think it simply won't work for you. But the truth is… energy is like gravity - it works whether you believe in it or not.

So why not figure out how it can work for you?

Maybe you believe that you don't have time for this.

The beautiful part of the Quantum Now is that it only takes a moment once you know the way. Everybody has at least a few moments each day to connect to the One Consciousness, and taking such a small amount of time to go through the seven steps *will* positively affect the rest of your day.

At this moment, right here and now, dear reader, you really have three options:

The first option is just to continue connecting with energy in the way that you are now. You could close this book, call it all nonsense, and go on living your life believing that you are not in control of positively affecting your mindset, exuberance, or acceptance of the things happening around you. If that's working for you, then chances are you wouldn't have made it this far anyway. You want change - you want to harness the power that resides within you.

The second option is to experiment with the energy on your own. You can take all of the information within these pages and see how it works in your life. That is certainly possible, though there is a huge difference between simply learning these tenets and knowing when and how to implement them. That's not to say that it cannot be done alone; after all, I figured it out. But it took a long time. Decades! Why not fast-track the process, avoiding all the potential pitfalls and mistakes you will inevitably make?

That leads us to our third (best) option: learning to harness the energy with a master teacher as your guide. When the student is ready, the teacher appears.

This teacher is ready… are you?

≹

A student and dear friend, Kato Crow, came into our QEI program ready to let go of decades of trauma. In her words, "From outside appearances, I looked pretty good, but on the inside, I had some stinkin' thinkin', shame triggers, and was raised with generational family dysfunction, abuse, and secrets.

I started QEI interested in the chakras because I knew what they were but had never studied them. Along with our Quantum Quickies, I felt better Immediately! QEI systematically built insights and knowledge on top of each lesson.

The next tools for releasing trapped emotions were exactly what I had been missing. Productive tears! I experienced relief each time I faced my shadows/fears, released the muckety-muck into the universe, and grounded it down into Mother Earth. Connie cautioned us about "growing pains." I used naps and nature to recalibrate regularly.

I had been working on self-care and moved into self-love. My favorite energetic states are Clearing and Charging. It is so cleansing to let go of the old trauma and then fill myself up with LifeForce Energy. I use the Chakra Charge every day.

Now, I have a daily energy practice, and I'm a beneficial presence on the planet. My self-love has advanced to self-reverence, and I'm confident and empowered, knowing Everything is Energy."

If you've read this far, you likely have a clear picture of what a Quantum Now Practice looks like, but perhaps you're not sure if it's right for your life. To help you figure that out, I've created **The Quantum Now Quiz** so you can get an idea of where you are energetically right now. Remember that your thoughts and feelings are energy, too!

If you're ready to harness the power of the present to find your purpose and live the life you haven't dared to desire, go to QuantumNowBook.com.

❧

I want you to know that I struggled for years with indecision, poor health, bad decisions, addictions, and personal trauma affecting the quality of my life.

It took a near-death experience for me to get serious about taking charge of my life. Of all the things I studied, the courses I took, and the degrees I earned, learning about energy is what changed my life.

Regardless of where you go from here, always remember that

everything is energy, *and so are you.*

If we want to create a more positive and sustainable future, it is essential that we understand that everything is energy. This understanding can help us to live more in harmony with ourselves, each other, and the planet.

If you'd like to book an Energy Breakthrough Session with me to discover at least one new way to expand your energy, go to QuantumNowBook.com.

One way or another, dear reader, I invite you not to allow any more precious moments to pass you by. The Quantum Now is always here, there, and everywhere, but you must engage with it, or you will find yourself drowning at 30,000 feet, just like I did.

Thank goodness that angel came to help me breathe in the LifeForce Energy that kept me alive on the plane. That angel, whose name was John, was a dear friend of mine who had just passed away two months earlier.

Everything is energy, even angels!

A NOTE FROM
"QUANTUM CONNIE"

I love the nickname Quantum Connie. My editor gave it to me when we were writing this book. She noticed the side of me readers may not see; she called it "an infectious, playful, vibrant and *loveable* energy that is at once calming and invigorating." She even made me buy QuantumConnie.com so I could use it to tell people how they could reach out to me directly.

I was called to write this book so I could share some simple, fast-acting, powerful tools to live your not-so-simple life with focus and grace.

The Quantum Now Practice is an integral part of my daily life. It is a beautiful life full of love from family and friends, highs and lows being an entrepreneur building a company, and personal challenges and devastating losses that I do not let define me.

I've come a long way since 1978 –yes, I've been at this for a very long time! It's been several decades since those dark days right after my brother died when I was suffocating from grief, when I decided to go right back to graduate school far away from my family, when I used alcohol and sex to drown out my pain, and when I hid who I was because I was so ashamed of my addictions.

It was a lonely, depressing, terrifying time when I had to hit rock bottom to stop the self-abuse and find some help. Some of the techniques I share in this book were born when I first stepped on that road to recovery.

Fast forward to my near-death experience in 1994 when, in my search for restoring my health from pneumonia, I started my adventure into energy. The next "quantum leap" in my life happened on 12/21/2012, the Winter Solstice, when the world was ending – or better stated – when a new era was ushered in. It felt like a huge energy shift for me and the planet.

It was then I started hearing and channeling ascended masters. At that time, my master teacher was Jesus. We had daily conversations for years where he hammered into me the principles of acceptance, non-judgment, and unconditional love. He spoke into the energies of the Celestial Realm and talked about the state of the Earthly Realm.

It was in 2014 that Jesus told me about "The Shift in Consciousness" for humanity that was coming, and it was going to happen in my lifetime! He said that it wouldn't take everyone – only enough of us, a critical mass, to raise our frequencies – so that all of humanity could shift into the consciousness of Love. He called it Heaven on Earth.

Jesus also talked a lot about 5th-dimensional energies that were coming through those of us who were ready to do the work. He made it very clear to me that everyone who was needed for The

Shift had already incarnated for this unprecedented up-leveling of humanity.

Since then, my mission has been to Raise the Collective Consciousness to Peaceful CoExistence. Everything I teach and have created works towards this bigger vision of our loving, accepting world.

When we understand that everything is energy, even you and me, we can use the Quantum Now Practice to uplevel our lives. We have a simple yet powerful system that helps us shift our energetic states, clear out old, slower-vibrating blockages, and bring in higher-vibrating LifeForce Energy to raise the frequency of our bodies.

All of this, dear Reader, is for you to have an energy system in place so you can raise your own frequency to the consciousness of Love.

With enough of us doing just this, we can shift the entire collective consciousness to Love and peacefully coexist on our beautiful Mother Earth.

To all the energy that is you,
Quantum Connie

ACKNOWLEDGMENTS

I am grateful to each of you who showed up in my life as a student, a teacher, a friend, a client, or a colleague who has helped me evolve into who I am today.

I am especially grateful to my children, Chad and Torie, who grew up with a mom who was really different and they loved me fully. They are my guiding lights.

I am grateful for my grandchildren who are walking, talking light stations that constantly remind me of how pure our energy truly is. They are like sponges when working with the energy and are showing me the way to design the programs for QEI Kids.

I am grateful for Jim, my partner of 38 years, who believed in me even when others called me "the crazy lady next door." He was a chemical engineer who took the Reiki and tapping and meditation classes when I asked him to so we could talk about energy together. Connecting in the energy deepened our relationship. He was my rock.

I am so grateful for my parents, Doris and Larry Chadwick,

who "raised me right." It wasn't their fault that I didn't fit into that mold of the '50s and '60s. They loved me even when they didn't understand me.

I am grateful to my book coach, Lin Eleoff, who heard my message, helped me put words around it, didn't give up on me, laughed with me, and turned me into an author.

I acknowledge all of you who show up every day shining your light and bringing your gifts to the world. Because of you, we are Raising the Collective Consciousness to Peaceful CoExistence.

ABOUT THE AUTHOR

Connie Kean is a cutting-edge Energy Consultant, Instructor, and Speaker with a history of life-changing successes in transformational energy work.

Connie built Quantum Energy Infusion (QEI), an international educational platform, by incorporating decades of experience as an Energy Practitioner and Reiki Master with her talents as a professional musician whose 40-year career focused on teaching piano, music theory, and performance.

QEI also demonstrates how to clear, strengthen, and balance the major energy systems within the body. QEI students and clients unanimously report better sleep, less pain, more energy, and reduced stress during and after completing the QEI program.

Connie takes great pride in instructing students on practical energy techniques so they can experience life as it comes in the present moment. Her fascination with the power of the present moment is the foundation of The Quantum Now Practice.

As the founder of QEI, Connie is dedicated to spreading the message that *everything is energy* and encourages everyone she meets to engage with the Quantum Field. Her mission is to Raise the Collective Consciousness to Peaceful CoExistence.

Learn more about Connie Kean and the Quantum Energy Infusion programs at https://www.quantumenergyinfusion. com.

The Quantum Now

By Connie Kean

QuantumNowBook.com

QuantumEnergyInfusion.com

QuantumConnie.com

Published by AFGO Press
AFGOpress.com

Made in the USA
Columbia, SC
17 November 2023

26653192R00057